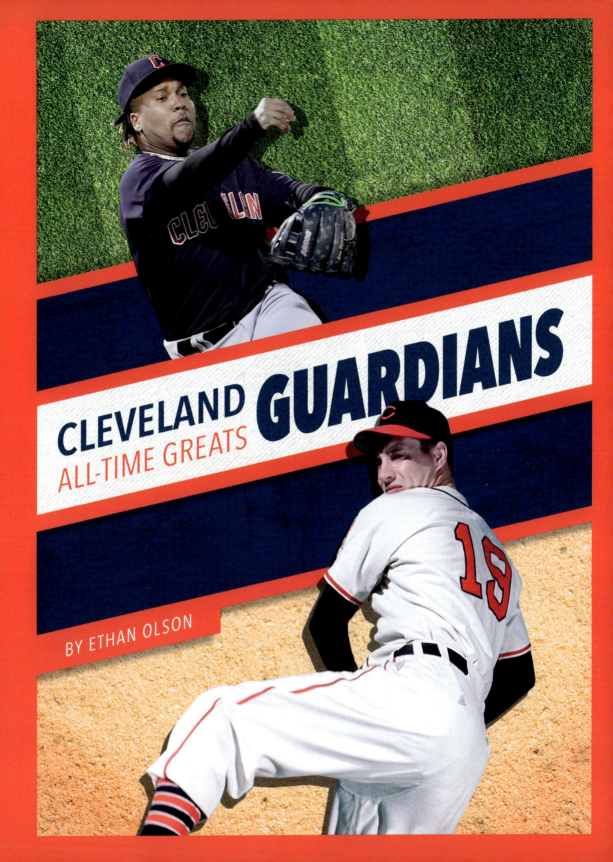

CLEVELAND GUARDIANS
ALL-TIME GREATS

BY ETHAN OLSON

Copyright © 2024 by Press Room Editions. All rights reserved. No part of this book may be used or reproduced in any manner whatsoever, including internet usage, without written permission from the copyright owner, except in the case of brief quotations embodied in critical articles and reviews.

Book design by Jake Slavik
Cover design by Jake Slavik

Photographs ©: Jeff Chiu/AP Images, cover (top), 1 (top); AP Images, cover (bottom), 1 (bottom); Transcendental Graphics/Getty Images Sport/Getty Images, 4; Bruce Bennett/Getty Images, 7; Mark Rucker/Transcendental Graphics/Getty Images Sport/Getty Images, 8; Bettmann/Getty Images, 10, 13, 15; Focus On Sport/Getty Images Sport/Getty Images, 16; Chuck Rydlewski/Getty Images Sport/Getty Images, 19; Ron Schwane/Getty Images Sport/Getty Images, 21

Press Box Books, an imprint of Press Room Editions.

ISBN
978-1-63494-794-7 (library bound)
978-1-63494-814-2 (paperback)
978-1-63494-852-4 (epub)
978-1-63494-834-0 (hosted ebook)

Library of Congress Control Number: 2023910366

Distributed by North Star Editions, Inc.
2297 Waters Drive
Mendota Heights, MN 55120
www.northstareditions.com

Printed in the United States of America
012024

ABOUT THE AUTHOR
Ethan Olson is a sportswriter and editor based in Minneapolis.

TABLE OF CONTENTS

CHAPTER 1
FOREVER CLEVELAND 5

CHAPTER 2
PERFECT PITCHING 11

CHAPTER 3
GUARDIANS OF CLEVELAND 17

TIMELINE 22
TEAM FACTS 23
MORE INFORMATION 23
GLOSSARY 24
INDEX 24

CHAPTER 1
FOREVER CLEVELAND

The Cleveland Guardians' story began when the American League (AL) started in 1901. They were originally known as the Cleveland Blues. By 1903, they were called the Naps.

This name came from early star **Nap Lajoie**. The second baseman arrived from the Philadelphia Athletics in 1902 and brought thousands of new fans to Cleveland's games. Lajoie quickly became the team captain and Cleveland's manager in 1905. Lajoie was a solid manager. But he was a far better player. He won four batting titles with Cleveland.

Addie Joss starred next to Lajoie. The dynamic pitcher had the lowest earned run average (ERA) in the AL in 1904. Joss was even better in 1908. His 1.16 ERA was the lowest in the league once again. And late in the year, he threw the fourth perfect game in Major League Baseball (MLB) history. Joss finished his career with a 1.89 ERA, which is tied for the second lowest in MLB history.

As Lajoie got older, **Shoeless Joe Jackson** became Cleveland's star hitter. Jackson got the nickname after batting with his shoes off in an amateur game. He burst onto the AL scene in 1911 with a .408 batting average. Jackson followed that up by leading the AL in hits in 1912 and 1913. In five seasons with Cleveland, Jackson was one of the AL's most consistent hitters.

JACKSON

Lajoie left Cleveland after the 1914 season. So the team needed a new name. Starting in the 1915 season, it went by the Indians. Pitcher **Stan Coveleski** was a focal point of the new era. Hitters struggled to make contact against the righty. He led the AL in strikeouts in 1920.

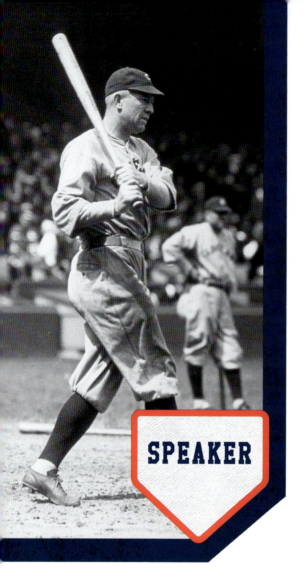

In that year's World Series, Coveleski won all three games he started and allowed only two runs. That helped Cleveland win its first MLB title.

Tris Speaker was the manager and center fielder of the title-winning team. In that year's World Series, he racked

STAT SPOTLIGHT

MOST CAREER DOUBLES
MLB RECORD
Tris Speaker: 792

ONE PLAYER, THREE OUTS

Cleveland second baseman Bill Wambsganss made history in Game 5 of the 1920 World Series. He caught a line drive with runners at first and second. The batter was out. Then Wambsganss stepped on second base for the second out. Next, he tagged the lead runner for the third out. More than a century later, it was still the only triple play ever turned in the baseball postseason.

up eight hits in seven games. Throughout his Hall of Fame career, Speaker constantly hit the ball into the outfield gaps. He led the AL in doubles in six different seasons with Cleveland.

Joe Sewell joined Cleveland late in the 1920 season. For the next 11 years, Sewell was a steady presence at the plate. He got on base a ton. And it was nearly impossible to strike Sewell out. He fanned only 99 times in 1,513 games with Cleveland.

CHAPTER 2
PERFECT PITCHING

In 1929, **Earl Averill** hit a home run in his first MLB at-bat. The center fielder kept on hitting for the next decade. Averill topped 30 home runs in three separate seasons.

Righthander **Bob Feller** was still in high school when he made his first start in 1936. Two years later, he was only 19 when he led the AL with 308 strikeouts. Feller continued

STAT SPOTLIGHT

MOST CAREER STRIKEOUTS
GUARDIANS TEAM RECORD
Bob Feller: 2,581

frustrating hitters until 1941. That year he became the first MLB player to sign up for military service in World War II (1939–45). After the war, "Rapid Robert" returned to Cleveland and went right back to work. He struck out 348 batters in 1946, which was an MLB single-season record at the time.

Bob Lemon started his career as a utility player. He didn't become a full-time pitcher until 1948. It was a good move for Lemon, as he won 20 games that year. Lemon repeated that feat five more times.

Larry Doby joined Cleveland in 1947, just months

BREAKING BARRIERS

Larry Doby broke barriers on the field in Cleveland. Later, Frank Robinson broke barriers in the dugout. Robinson became Cleveland's manager in 1975. This made him the first Black manager in the history of MLB.

after Jackie Robinson broke baseball's color barrier. The center fielder was the first Black player in the AL. Starting in 1949, he was an All-Star for seven straight seasons.

Lou Boudreau was Cleveland's star shortstop in the 1940s. In 1942, he also became the team's manager. Boudreau won the AL's Most Valuable Player (MVP) Award in 1948. More importantly, he led the team to the World Series that year. Cleveland won another title by taking down the Boston Braves in six games.

Legendary Boston Red Sox hitter Ted Williams once said **Early Wynn** was the toughest pitcher he ever faced. It's not hard to understand why. The reliable righty led the AL with a 3.20 ERA in 1950.

While Wynn was dominating at the mound, third baseman **Al Rosen** was doing so at the plate. In 1953, he had career highs of 43 home runs and 145 runs batted in (RBIs). That earned Rosen the AL MVP.

CHAPTER 3
GUARDIANS OF CLEVELAND

After a World Series loss in 1954, Cleveland fell into a major slump. The team didn't make the playoffs for decades. But the presence of slugger **Jim Thome** helped turn things around. After making his debut in 1991, the infielder became one of the most feared hitters in baseball. Starting in 1996, Thome hit more than 30 home runs for seven straight seasons with Cleveland.

Kenny Lofton started his career in Cleveland with a bang. As a rookie in 1992, Lofton stole 66 bases. That led the AL and broke the team record for most in a season.

Lofton's speed also helped him in center field, as he often made spectacular catches.

The emergence of **Manny Ramírez** pushed Cleveland to the next level. In 1995, the right fielder helped the team make the playoffs for the first time in 41 years. Cleveland made it all the way to the World Series in 1995 and in 1997. However, both ended in losses. Ramírez still thrived each season after those disappointments. In 1999, he racked up 165 RBIs. That made him the first player since 1938 to have more than 160 RBIs in a season.

STAT SPOTLIGHT

MOST CAREER HOME RUNS
GUARDIANS TEAM RECORD
Jim Thome: 337

CC Sabathia became Cleveland's new ace in 2001. The 6-foot-6 (198 cm), 300-pound (136 kg) lefty overpowered hitters. In 2007, Sabathia won the Cy Young Award. This award goes to the best pitcher in each league every year.

Corey Kluber eventually became the team's new ace. By 2014, the righty was one of the best pitchers in baseball. Kluber used his devastating breaking ball to win the

AL Cy Young in both 2014 and 2017. His pitching helped lead Cleveland back to the World Series in 2016. However, the team lost Game 7 at home to the Chicago Cubs.

José Ramírez helped keep Cleveland a contender after the World Series loss. The third baseman's combination of power, speed, and defense made him one of baseball's best players. Cleveland fans hoped Ramírez could be the player to bring the city its first title since 1948.

> **A NEW ERA**
> For decades, the Indians nickname received criticism for being racially insensitive to Native Americans. That led to the team changing its name to the Guardians for the 2022 season. The new name was inspired by two statues on a bridge in Cleveland that are known as the "Guardians of Traffic."

TIMELINE

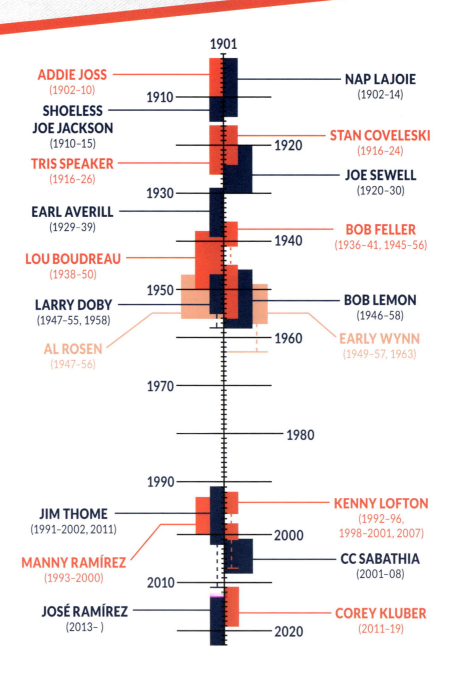

TEAM FACTS

CLEVELAND GUARDIANS

Team history: Cleveland Blues (1901), Cleveland Bronchos (1902), Cleveland Naps (1903-14), Cleveland Indians (1915-2021), Cleveland Guardians (2022-)

World Series titles: 2 (1920, 1948)*

Key managers:

Lou Boudreau (1942-50)
728-649-12 (.529), 1 World Series title

Terry Francona (2013-)
845-671 (.557)

Tris Speaker (1919-26)
617-520 (.543), 1 World Series title

MORE INFORMATION
To learn more about the Cleveland Guardians, go to **pressboxbooks.com/AllAccess**.

These links are routinely monitored and updated to provide the most current information available.

*through 2022

GLOSSARY

ace
The best starting pitcher on a team.

amateur
Having to do with players who are not paid.

consistent
Reliable, unchanging.

debut
First appearance.

dynamic
Energetic, creating positive change.

rookie
A first-year player.

slump
A period where a team or player isn't performing up to expectations.

utility player
A player who can play several different positions.

INDEX

Averill, Earl, 11

Boudreau, Lou, 14

Coveleski, Stan, 7–8

Doby, Larry, 12–13

Feller, Bob, 11–12

Jackson, Shoeless Joe, 6
Joss, Addie, 6

Kluber, Corey, 19–20

Lajoie, Nap, 5–7
Lemon, Bob, 12
Lofton, Kenny, 17–18

Ramírez, José, 20

Ramírez, Manny, 18
Rosen, Al, 14

Sabathia, CC, 19
Sewell, Joe, 9
Speaker, Tris, 8–9

Thome, Jim, 17–18

Wambsganss, Bill, 9
Wynn, Early, 14